IT'S TIME TO EAT
ALFALFA SPROUTS

It's Time to Eat ALFALFA SPROUTS

Walter the Educator

Silent King Books
A WhichHead Entertainment Imprint

Copyright © 2024 by Walter the Educator

All rights reserved. No part of this book may be reproduced in any manner whatsoever without written per- mission except in the case of brief quotations embodied in critical articles and reviews.

First Printing, 2024

Disclaimer

This book is a literary work; the story is not about specific persons, locations, situations, and/or circumstances unless mentioned in a historical context. Any resemblance to real persons, locations, situations, and/or circumstances is coincidental. This book is for entertainment and informational purposes only. The author and publisher offer this information without warranties expressed or implied. No matter the grounds, neither the author nor the publisher will be accountable for any losses, injuries, or other damages caused by the reader's use of this book. The use of this book acknowledges an understanding and acceptance of this disclaimer.

It's Time to Eat ALFALFA SPROUTS is a collectible early learning book by Walter the Educator suitable for all ages belonging to Walter the Educator's Time to Eat Book Series. Collect more books at WaltertheEducator.com

USE THE EXTRA SPACE TO TAKE NOTES AND DOCUMENT YOUR MEMORIES

ALFALFA SPROUTS

It's time to eat, hooray, hooray!

It's Time to Eat Alfalfa Sprouts

Alfalfa sprouts are on the way.

So tiny and light, they're fun to see,

A crunchy snack for you and me!

They're soft and curly, like little threads,

Topped on sandwiches or salads instead.

A sprinkle here, a handful there,

Alfalfa sprouts go everywhere!

They're grown in water, not in the ground,

In just a few days, they sprout all around.

With sunshine bright and water clear,

They grow to bring us tasty cheer!

Put them on toast or in a wrap,

Alfalfa sprouts give food a zap!

So fresh and crisp, a burst of green,

They make your plate look like a dream.

It's Time to Eat Alfalfa Sprouts

Crunch, crunch, crunch, that's their sound,

Tiny sprouts that truly astound.

A little bite, so fresh and bright,

Eating alfalfa feels just right!

They're full of goodness, did you know?

They help your body work and grow.

Sprouts are tiny, but oh so strong,

They'll keep you healthy all day long.

Imagine they're strings on a little harp,

Playing music that's crunchy and sharp.

But instead of a tune, they sing to you,

"Alfalfa sprouts are good for you!"

Sprinkle them high, sprinkle them low,

On eggs, on rice, or in tacos, oh!

It's Time to Eat Alfalfa Sprouts

No matter the dish, they're always a treat,

Alfalfa sprouts are fun to eat!

So grab your fork, it's time to try,

These curly sprouts that never lie.

They'll make you smile with every bite,

A healthy snack that feels so right!

Thank you, sprouts, for being so neat,

For making our meals fresh and sweet.

We love alfalfa, small and true,

It's Time to Eat Alfalfa Sprouts

The perfect snack for me and you!

ABOUT THE CREATOR

Walter the Educator is one of the pseudonyms for Walter Anderson. Formally educated in Chemistry, Business, and Education, he is an educator, an author, a diverse entrepreneur, and he is the son of a disabled war veteran. "Walter the Educator" shares his time between educating and creating. He holds interests and owns several creative projects that entertain, enlighten, enhance, and educate, hoping to inspire and motivate you. Follow, find new works, and stay up to date with Walter the Educator™ at WaltertheEducator.com

www.ingramcontent.com/pod-product-compliance
Lightning Source LLC
LaVergne TN
LVHW052010060526
838201LV00059B/3949